Veterans in Consulting

~ A Guide to Help Military Veterans Evaluate and Pursue a Career in Management Consulting ~

Justin M. Nassiri

Veterans in Consulting: A Guide to Help Military Veterans Evaluate and Pursue a Career in Management Consulting

ISBN: 9781977014313

Cover creation by Creativelog Design

Formatting and editing by Lorraine Reguly

Table of Contents

To my third-grade teacher, Brenda, who taught me how and encouraged me to write; who was always my most enthusiastic cheerleader; who gave me the confidence to "dare to be different."

I wouldn't be where I am without your constant love and support.

Introduction

In the 150+ interviews of U.S. Military Veterans that I have conducted with *Beyond the Uniform*, I have found two things to be true. **The first is that U.S. Military Veterans can do absolutely any civilian career imaginable.** Their military experience and skills honed while in the Armed Forces close no doors, and in many ways uniquely prepares them to pursue an incredibly diverse range of career options. However, the second truth I have observed is that **most Veterans drastically underestimate what it will take to pursue their desired career.**

My intention with this book – as with *Beyond the Uniform* – is to provide U.S. Military Veterans with the information, tools, and advice necessary to identify, pursue, and succeed at their ideal civilian career. If you read this book and decide that Management Consulting is not a career path you would like to pursue, that is just as much a victory as identifying it as your next career choice. As my career counselor, Andy Chen, told me at the Stanford Graduate School of Business: "Don't worry about finding out what you want to do. Start figuring out what you don't want to do, and start closing those doors."

This book is based on a quantitative analysis of over 4300 LinkedIn profiles of U.S. Military Veterans who have worked in the field of Management Consulting. It is also based on over ten hours of qualitative interviews with U.S. Military Veterans who have worked in the field of Management Consulting. I have combined everything that I know about this space and its compatibility with a U.S. Military Veteran with the hope that it provides you with the knowledge to decide how this career path may align with your unique interests, desires, and skill set.

As Master Chief Granito would always tell us on the USS Alaska: "Knowledge is power." I hope this knowledge takes you one step closer to finding the ideal career that you deserve.

How this Book is Structured

I have structured this book to first cover the more qualitative aspects of Management Consulting – why you may like this career, what it is, how that translates to a daily and weekly lifestyle, etc. For this section of the book, I have relied upon the qualitative interviews I have conducted through *Beyond the Uniform*.

The second portion of this book focuses on more quantitative analysis, based on a statistical analysis of public profiles on LinkedIn. My reasoning for this approach to data analysis is that, while few take the time to complete surveys, nearly all professionals in the civilian sector have an updated and accurate LinkedIn profile. Thus, this seems to be the most comprehensive and accurate database of Veteran information available as of the time of this writing.

It is worth noting that my intention for providing this data is simply to inform. In the 150+ interviews I have conducted for *Beyond the Uniform*, I have seen that there is no single path to any career destination. Veterans are capable of forging their own way and setting their own path. However, I do believe it is valuable to at least understand that path that many other Veterans have taken in pursuing a career in Management Consulting. So, I hope that this information is helpful – but not limiting – in your consideration of a career in Management Consulting.

Who I Interviewed for this Book

I refer frequently to conversations with a few people, and I would like to give you their background upfront so you can factor that in to the advice they provide. The three individuals I relied upon the most went directly from Active Duty to Management Consulting at one of the three biggest consulting companies, commonly called The Big Three: McKinsey & Company, The Boston Consulting Group, and Bain & Company.

As you will learn, less than 4% of all Veterans in Management Consulting are able to work at one of these companies, and only 7% of these people are able to go directly from Active Duty to Management Consulting. My intention in focusing on these perspectives is that – since this appears to be the most difficult path to achieve – the advice given by these individuals is likely of the highest quality and from the most rigorously earned experience.

Here are the people I will reference in this book:

Blake Lindsay is a Consultant for McKinsey & Company in their Denver office. He started out at the Naval Academy, then served as a nuclear qualified Surface Warfare Officer in the Navy for five years. While on Active Duty, Blake went through Old Dominion University's graduate school, then received his Master's in Engineering Management shortly after separating from the Navy.

Kristen Sproat Colley is a Consultant for the Boston Consulting Group (BCG) in their D.C. office. She started out at the U.S. Naval Academy and earned an MSc (Master of Science) from Oxford University in Forced Migration. She served as an officer in the U.S. Marine Corps for eight years, prior to making her transition to BCG.

Trevor Miller is a Consultant for Bain & Company in their Boston office. He started out at the U.S. Naval Academy, after which he earned his Master of Public Administration at Harvard University's John F. Kennedy School of Government. He served in the Marine Corps as a Force Reconnaissance Officer for six years before transitioning to Bain.

Eric Hulbert is a Consultant at the Boston Consulting Group in their Atlanta Office. He started out at the Naval Academy, then served for over 11 years as a pilot. After his transition from the military, Eric worked in the Finance Industry at Bank of America – as a Vice Principal of Strategy Analyst. Eric holds an MBA and a Master of Science in Industrial & Systems Engineering from the University of Florida

Timothy Avery faced his transition to civilian life much earlier than anticipated, and found himself – far ahead of his peer set – having to decide what to do. Initially, he found his way to Management Consulting, where he worked with both BearingPoint and Booz Allen Hamilton. After that, he transitioned to a doctoral program in clinical psychology (i.e., Doctorate of Psychology, or PsyD).

Tom Spahn has spent time in his civilian career as both a Corporate Lawyer at Sullivan & Cromwell, as well as a Management Consultant at McKinsey & Co. He has a collection of degrees – he received his Juris Doctor (JD) from Stanford Law School while simultaneously obtaining MSc in Management Science & Engineering. He also holds a Master in Engineering Management from Old Dominion University. Tom graduated from the Naval Academy and served on submarines with the crew of the USS Chicago (SSN 721).

Why Consulting?

In 2016, I analyzed over 5000 LinkedIn profiles of U.S. Military Veterans to determine trends in what this population does after their military service. As far as I know, it is the first research of its kind. One thing I realized during this process is that **Management Consulting is the 5th largest industry that members of the Armed Forces enter into after their military service.**

Why would a member of the Armed Forces consider starting his/her career in Management Consulting? For one thing, it is a very quick way for a Veteran to rapidly gain insight around a variety of industries and functional roles. Typically, Management Consultants will spend 2-12 months on a project. During this time, they dive deep within the company and work to solve an incredibly complex problem. By doing this, in the span of two years, Veterans could get an understanding of what industries they may like, and what functional roles may suit them.

That's what first attracted me to Consulting. When I served onboard nuclear submarines, I had very little insight into what I might do after my service, or even what career options were available. However, from those who had gone before me, I knew of one trend: military to business school, then business school to Management Consulting. The sense I got was that business school would fill in the gaps in my academic knowledge about business, and Management Consulting would round that out with the hands-on experience and exposure to all the routes I might then pursue.

For many of the Veterans I have interviewed, this rings true. During their time in Management Consulting, they started to get the sense of what industries they like. (Do they get energized by finance, pharmaceuticals, non-profits, or consumer packaged goods?) They started to get the feel for which functional areas sparked their curiosity. (Is it marketing, finance, or operations?) The rapid exposure to broad swathes of business experience seems like an ideal follow-up to a sustained period of service in the military.

This has been the case with Kristen Sproat Colley, who shared:

> "I think that's my favorite part about it. I've been able to try out a bunch of different things and decide what my passion is. There are so many different types of problems. Every client and every project is different. So, it's never the same thing twice. It's always a new set of problems and a new set of analysis that needs to be done."

A second reason that Management Consulting may to appeal to U.S. Military Veterans is that **the Management Consulting industry shares several characteristics with the military.** Mainly, it has a great training program and a fairly standardized career progression, just like the military. For those who want to minimize the amount of change in their lives as they shift from the world of Active Duty to the civilian world, Management Consulting may provide a more feasible stepping stone.

Additionally, **Management Consulting can teach Veterans extremely valuable frameworks for sorting through exceptionally complex challenges.** This skill set is likely to be highly valued in whatever eventual career a Veteran pursues (assuming they do not remain as a Management Consultant for their entire career). I appreciated Trevor Miller's perspective on this, when he told me:

> "Yes, I've definitely learned in consulting that this is a valuable way to look at problems. To take a structured approach, take a step back, and look at your different options. It can be uncomfortable because it's not what Veterans are used to but that discomfort can be very valuable."

One of the things I appreciated about my experience in the military was the level of responsibility I was given very early on in my career. When I was a 22-year-old, newly-qualified Officer of the Deck, I remember being in charge of our submarine and standing watch at 2 AM, wondering, *Who on earth let me do this?!?* **Management Consulting can similarly supply rapid access to**

high-growth opportunities and situations. As Blake Lindsay put it:

> "You build a skill set that's very valuable, because you are constantly punching above your weight class. I have thirty minutes before I have a meeting with the president of a Fortune 500 company. And that's not an uncommon occurrence. If I was working in the corporate world, it would take me a long time to get that type of experience."

The final advantage of this career path is that Management Consulting does not seem to close any doors. It is a valuable skill set that can be beneficial – no matter what your eventual career is. Tim Avery, who faced an unexpected early transition from the military, became interested in Consulting for two specific reasons:

> "Since it was my first job out of the military, I really wanted to keep my options open and not be pigeon-holed into a certain role within a company. At the same time, I really wanted to increase my skills and knowledge. Consulting offered the best of both worlds – it allowed me to maintain and expand my career options, while at the same time teaching me concrete and valuable skills."

If you are uncertain about what you would like to do after your military service, Consulting can be an ideal path to narrowing in on where you would like to focus your career.

Let's now look at what exactly Consulting is.

What is Consulting?

As the fifth largest industry that members of the Armed Forces enter into after their military service, consulting offers a strong appeal to Veterans. But what exactly is it?

As Kristen Sproat Colley put it:

> "At its core, Consulting is about coming up with optimal solutions for messy and complex problems. We generally know the approximate problem and then we do an in-depth analysis to figure out the root of the problem. We then come up with different courses of action to solve those problems through evidence and data. We make those recommendations to decision-makers within the organization. The whole process is actually quite similar to the military planning process."

As you'll see in the chapter on interviewing, because of the need to solve complex problems in a variety of situations, the application and interview process for Management Consulting can be extremely demanding. When I spoke with Blake Lindsay, he described it this way:

> "We develop long-term, long-standing relationships with big, major clients – all of the largest companies in the world. We help them to solve their biggest problems, help guide them through changes in markets and industries, help them weather storms, and set strategic directions that allows them to continue to succeed in the way that they always have."

This can be one of the more rewarding aspects of a career in Management Consulting – you are constantly at the cutting-edge of business, working with high-caliber companies on their toughest challenges. In this sense, it seems like an equivalent "tip of the spear" scenario, but in the civilian business sector.

When I interviewed Trevor Miller (who works for Bain & Company), he spoke to how his view of Consulting has changed the more he has been involved in it:

> "That's a great question that I thought I knew the answer to, but now that I'm here doing it every day, my perspective has evolved. At the most basic level, a Management Consultant is an advisor. The role that you take as an advisor can vary significantly in terms of function or industry. But generally speaking, Bain focuses on helping clients with strategy-level questions. If you're making a military analogy, you're talking about strategy planning. These are plans that have the potential to be implemented over several years but could have even longer time horizons. They're generally thorny issues, which is a reason why consultants are brought in. There are many cases where it helps to get a third party's point of view. So that's what we do – we take a very data-driven look at an issue and then provide recommendations for ways forward. Sometimes, we'll help them action it but, really, they are set up to be able to do that themselves."

Tom Spahn had an interesting view on Management Consulting, as he worked as an attorney prior to starting at McKinsey & Company. As he contrasted his two career paths, he really appreciated the creativity that he associates with consulting work:

> "With consulting, quite often, it is a wide-open problem. A company asks you to solve Problem X and they brought you in because they may not have been able to solve it themselves, because it is the most difficult problem. And you have *carte blanche* to propose a solution and come up with an answer that satisfies the need."

While many Veterans may not recognize it, there have been circumstances in the military that use a consulting-style approach. When I was serving on the USS Alaska as the Damage Control Assistant, I was tasked with overhauling our equipment defect management system. In retrospect, I realize that this was essentially a consulting project, for the following reasons:

- I had to meet with key stakeholders on the crew to better understand the problem.
- I had to identify what was causing the problem and come up with solutions.
- I had to present my findings to our Captain and senior leaders.
- Then I had to sell the solution to our crew and help them implement it.

Seeing one's military experience in this light may help you understand that **Management Consulting is not as unfamiliar as one might initially think.** And, as we'll learn in the Interviewing section, being able to explain one's military background through the lens of consulting will be essential to getting the job.

Now that we've discussed what it is to be a Management Consultant, let's zoom in and see what this translates to on a day-to-day and week-to-week basis.

Hours & Lifestyle

When I speak with Veterans about their civilian career, there tends to be three areas of concern for them. **The first is the number of hours that they will need to work** each week in their new role. **The second is the amount of travel** that a job will entail and how this may impact their weekends. **And the third is their overall work-life balance.** These are all important aspects to consider when evaluating any career.

Hours Per Week

When I spoke with Trevor Miller about the hours he works each week, his answer seemed consistent with what I have heard from more than a dozen others:

> "Numbers-wise, I'd say that 60-70 hours a week is typical. The way that I do that is that I do five 12-hour days, sometimes more than 12 hours a day, since Friday is usually a bit shorter."

Blake Lindsay added some color to this answer by taking me through his typical day:

> "When I'm traveling and on the road, it's pretty easy to put in a long day. My regular day is that I'm up at 5:00 or 5:30 AM and do my workouts in the morning. I'm into the office around 7:30 and usually stay in the office until around 6:30 or 7:30 PM, working with my team. Then I go and I eat, and usually end up working a couple more hours after that – answering emails, creating presentations for conversations I'm going to have with clients the next day, and that sort of thing. So, I'm working 13-15 hour days pretty frequently, Monday through Thursday."

However, of all of the comments I heard in the dozens of interviews I conducted, the insight that Trevor Miller shared with me stuck with me the most. While Veterans tend to focus on the hours per week a job may entail, they may be overlooking the extreme difference between the quality of workstyle they are accustomed to in the military, and the quality of the workstyle associated with Management Consulting. As Trevor put it:

> "The difference to me is that I thought I knew what it meant to work a 60-hour week. I thought in the military I knew what it meant to work 24/7, having a deployment be my frame of reference. For me, the 60 hours of consulting work was *very* different than the 24/7 deployment work. When I was leading people deployed, there was a certain amount of intensity in brief moments. Like they say – war is hours of boredom punctuated by seconds of sheer terror. That, in some ways for me, was easier for me to handle than the exhaustion I feel from 60 hours of consulting. It's 60 hours of thinking critically, non-stop, where there's never any known solution or path to where you're going. "

It is important to also note that **companies can vary significantly in the amount that you work.** Tim Avery did consulting work at both BearingPoint and Booz Allen Hamilton. His experience was very different than that of Kristen, Blake, and Trevor. As Tim put it:

> "I was largely in federal practice where our client was the federal government. Our contracts were typically for the government workweek. We couldn't work more than 40 hours that were billable to the client. So, if I wasn't responsible for business development and bringing in new clients, my schedule really mirrored that of a government employee."

A Typical Day's Schedule

From my *Beyond the Uniform* podcast, I know that listeners really appreciate the granular detail of what a typical day looks like in a given job. As a result, I asked several Veterans to take me through their typical day. Each was quick to point out that there is no "typical day." However, given that, here is what they told me.

Eric Hulbert shared his typical day:

> "I leave the hotel around 7:15 AM and am at the client site by 8:00 AM. We work there until around 7:00 PM. The workday consists of team meetings where we discuss research we're doing and analysis we're doing, and slides we're making as a team. We'll have meetings with clients where we're brainstorming with them, getting data from them, showing them our findings so far, and getting their reaction. We'll also have formal team meetings. After we leave the client site around 7:00 PM, sometimes we'll stop somewhere and grab a quick dinner as a team. Once a week, we'll have a nice dinner as a team, where we go to a nice restaurant and stay there for 1.5-2 hours. And sometimes we'll just get back to the hotel and eat in our rooms. Most people take a bit of time to relax, and then get back to work and go from maybe 9:00-11:00 PM or so. And then *wince* and repeat! That's Monday through Thursday for me, and then back in the home office on Friday."

As she considered her time spent at The Boston Consulting Group, Kristen Sproat Colley described her daily life in this way:

> "It really varies depending on the project. We normally travel to the client site for 3-4 days during the week. It's very important to me that I maintain my morning workouts, even with travel. Usually, I'll travel to the client site early on a Monday morning and get there by 9 AM. I'll usually align with my manager and talk about what needs to get done. Then when I get time to start my work, usually I'll reach out to subject matter experts for an interview. I also have time when I sit down with the client and brainstorm or talk about possible solutions. Sometimes I'm working on slide content or with other members of the team. We usually get lunch together as a team and then, after lunch, I'll check back in with my manager. I keep working on content and analysis.

Typically we get together as a team for dinner. Then I go back to my hotel room and talk to my husband. I then continue to work until 11 or so."

Trevor Miller describes his daily life with Bain & Company in this way:

"There's a high degree of variance. I would put the typical day into two categories – one in which you're at the office and one in which you're away working on a case. In my experience, the day tends to be a bit earlier if you're away on a case. You usually have a team meeting in the morning to get everyone on the same page. You might be working on some sort of analysis or doing phone calls from the client site. You could be meeting with clients. In the afternoon, you generally check in with your team and see what kind of progress everyone is making. The majority of my cases have been local cases. Usually, with these cases, there's less client interaction, and you might be working at your desk in the office for most of the time. You truly are an individual contributor in many ways and there might be less team and client interaction than you may think."

Tom Spahn echoed the sentiment of the high amount of variability between one project and the next:

"You know generally what problem the client is trying to solve – or what problem they think they are trying to solve. So, step one is to make sure you're solving the right problem, and getting to the root of why the client thinks that is a problem. That can involve interviews with the senior management, that can be independent observations, it can be looking at data and creating Excel models, etc. Once you do that, there are tons of different ways to get to the solution. It's less about creating your own solution and more about co-creating a solution with your client, and making sure it's something the client will use going forward and can implement without us. Because, ultimately, our job is to work ourselves out of a job, and passing on the skills so the client can do it themselves."

Travel Schedule

When I've spoken with Veterans in Management Consultant, it appears that **travel is highly dependent on the company for which you work.** Some companies, for example, focus on local projects and have minimal travel. Others, however, can be much more notorious for travel. That said, it also became clear that **there is some choice in this matter,** even at the firms associated with a high rate of travel.

As you work with the Human Resources department at your company, you can prioritize the types of projects on which you would like to work. Is a particular industry the most important to you? Great – then they can help prioritize that for your next project. However, if travel is the most important factor, it seems likely that you can prioritize that aspect as you select your next project.

Here is an example of what a travel schedule may look like, as well as the types of activities that will fill your day. Reflecting on his experience at McKinsey & Company, Blake Lindsay had this to offer:

> "I typically travel Monday through Thursday, depending on where my client is located. I live in Denver, but I have a major client in Seattle, a major client in Philadelphia, and another major client in Texas. So, I am typically traveling to those places during the week to meet with my clients and work with them.
>
> I also lead a team of other Consultants. Typically, what we do is identify issues for our client and carve out how to work that issue. I help them solve the problem in a clear and distinct way and make recommendations on the backend of the engagement. I also work on the implementation aspect of

this work. I'm working side-by-side with my clients to help them setup a management structure and system which they can work through and go and tackle these problems. We measure our impact by dollars we are saving, or revenues that are being generated, or whatever the end goal is."

Weekends

One aspect that appears to be fairly consistent with consulting is that – while the workweek may be extremely demanding and may also require travel – **weekends generally seem to be well-respected boundaries.** In my view, this sets Management Consulting apart from other career paths I have interviewed for *Beyond the Uniform*, which generally seem to involve at least a few hours of work on the weekends.

That is certainly the case for Kristen Sproat Colley from the Boston Consulting Group, who told me:

> "Since I've been with BCG, I've only had to work two weekends. Usually I like to put in an hour or two on Sunday, just to plan my week. However, I have worked on projects overseas and the attitude changes a bit over there. But BCG is really good about letting people have a work-life balance. Part of it is also about setting boundaries for yourself."

Trevor Miller agrees with this, as he says:

> "I've been here [six months] and I have yet to work a weekend. I would say that in some people's case, that hasn't been the same. For me, I make it a point. One of the things that we do here when a team starts is that you share your priorities. For me it's a hard line that I'm not even going to look at my email over the weekend. I used to think about this mentality about being lazy or unmotivated. But it's something that I've committed myself during my time here and I've been able to strengthen my relationship with my

wife and kids. I think it even improves the quality of my work during the week because I know I have to focus on what I need to get done."

Blake Lindsay echoed these statements as well, but also emphasized the amount of personal choice involved in this:

"For me, it's incredibly rare to have to work on the weekend. This place is like anywhere else – it is a gas and it will fill the space that you provide it, and so I hard-stop at 5:00 PM on Friday. I do not re-engage until Monday morning, unless [it is] the rare time when I engage with someone on Sunday evening."

Tom Spahn talked about how he enjoyed the predictability of his schedule. He knows that on travel assignments, Monday through Thursday will be extremely busy, but that there is not much else to do while away from home anyways. Then, when he returns home on Thursday evening, he knows that Friday will be more relaxed, and his weekend will be untouched by work.

Work-life Balance and Boundaries

Each of the Veterans I interviewed described a similar process at the start of each and every consulting project. **Prior to beginning their new work together, the team would take the time for each member of the project to share their working style and priorities.** For example, one member might say that 5:00-6:00 PM each evening was sacred, a time for them to connect with their family back home. Others might mention that a morning run is key in their life, and that they like to keep 7:00-8:00 AM free for this activity.

I think this is a fantastic process. **Not only do you get to be clear on what matters most to you in your schedule, but you are allowed to communicate this to your coworkers so they can work around it.** In each interview, the Veterans mentioned that their groups have consistently been accommodating of these constraints. So, while the amount of work associated with consulting may be very high, at least you know that there is some choice in how that time is spent.

Now that we've zoomed in on what the day-to-day and week-to-week life looks like for a Consultant, let's look at a few specific examples of the types of projects on which you could work.

Sample Consulting Projects

In my research, I made a point to drill into specific examples of some of the projects each Veteran has worked on. It is standard in consulting that the exact client company is not mentioned by name. As a result, in each of these examples, the Veteran will refer to an industry or type of problem being solved, but cannot speak to the specific company with whom they worked.

Before diving into a few specific examples, I want to elaborate on the process through which you are assigned your new project. Kristen Sproat Colley's experience was representative of what I heard in other interviews:

> "Each consulting firm has a different model for staffing projects. At BCG, projects are typically anywhere from 2 weeks to 6 months. In terms of how I get those projects, we are a generalist firm. That means that when you first start, you can be assigned anywhere. When I came in, I had a good sense of the military but really wanted to work outside of that. The first couple [of] projects you work on are to develop your skill set but also focus you on what kind of projects you want to work on.
>
> We have a staffing coordinator that oversees everyone's assignments. I went to her and told her that I was interested in tech projects. She then put me in touch with who would be my project manager and I was able to talk to them about what the project would be like. You can then decide if the project is the right fit for you.
>
> For me, I specifically requested a project in the Middle East. I got staffed on a public-sector project that I really enjoyed. I'm currently in that matching process again now to find my next project."

Consultants are constantly going through this staffing process. As they find an industry, functional area, geography, or manager they like, they can choose to continue to focus on projects in that area. Narrowing in on an area of focus can lead to a tremendous amount of variety.

Eric Hulbert shared specific examples of his experience starting in Consulting, and how he has navigated his project selection so far:

> "When you're brand new, you don't know what you don't know, so I just took the first case they offered me. We worked with a large government agency to do transformation work – revising all of their processes, procedures, and structures to be a more modern organization.
>
> But for my second project, I told them I wanted to prioritize being with a manager who had a strong reputation for developing his team. And that's what they gave me and it worked out fantastically. That second project was with a large retail company to help with their inventory management and making sure they have better availability of products on their shelf.
>
> Now that I'm starting to get the hang of things, I'm starting to focus on an area that we call Customer Insights – surveying a company's customers, and researching to find out what they are actually looking for."

The process of narrowing in on an area of focus can be quite energizing. Tom Spahn spoke to the incredible diversity he has had in each of his Consulting projects at McKinsey & Company:

> "There's so much variety. I've done projects with aircraft manufacturing, where I was literally walking around an aircraft being built and helping improve the efficiency of cataloguing the parts. I spent a winter up at an arctic diamond mine, looking at mining operations in the frozen tundra. Now I'm working on a corporate restructuring, which is a mix of

law and operations. Every project I've done has been totally different from the last."

Blake Lindsay, who has had six years of Management Consulting experience (like most of those I have interviewed), talked about how he has started to specialize in Operations at McKinsey & Company. So, at this point in his career, his projects are more similar:

> "I work in the Operations Practice. I help organizations – typically who make something or provide some sort of service – figure out how to make or provide that service better, while reducing costs for their production facilities… all while helping the overall organization and culture improve through long-term strategic changes and initiatives."

Kristen Sproat Colley shared this story about one of her first consulting projects:

> "We were hired by a technology client that was interested in learning about different uses for blockchain. This is the same technology that is behind Bitcoin. The client understood blockchain, but applying it to international trade and shipping was a new application, and they wanted to understand how the two might come together. Our job was to learn about blockchain and how it could be used in global supply systems. We came up with both short and long-term pathways for the company.
>
> During the research period on the project, I visited a local shipyard to look at all the paperwork that goes along with incoming shipments. We put together some product ideas and made recommendations to the client about what they would need to do if they pursued particular routes.
>
> It was actually very similar to my experience as a Junior Officer in the military, where I wasn't a subject matter expert, but had to work with a team of various experts and then help create a solution.

This is a question faced a lot in consulting – you're an outsider and not part of the company. How can you solve a problem the company can't even solve themselves? It's not that we're smarter or more capable. It's that we can bring a different lens and focus. We get up to speed using resources from the company. We also work with the client to fill in our knowledge gaps. Then we come up with possible solutions, so it's really a problem-solving endeavor. The skill that we bring is being able to break down a complex problem into smaller pieces and offer solutions."

Kristen liked her work in the Middle East, and sought to do another project in the same geographic area that was very different than this first project:

"I worked for a United States defense company that was starting a Middle East subsidiary. They had been operating in the region for a while but there was a lot more business development that needed to happen. My team and I went in and helped them figure out the right strategy for meeting with and working with key stakeholders. And then we also made suggestions for what kinds of people would need to be on their team in order to successfully implement their strategy. We then worked with the CEO of the subsidiary to make recommendations and help him start implementing strategies."

Trevor Miller shared one of his favorite Consulting projects to date:

"I worked on a post-acquisition integration for a company that bought another company for over 6 billion [dollars]. We focused on how to improve this new, combined company without relying on reducing headcount to lower their costs. By the end of the project, we were able to lower their costs by over 200 million [dollars], and were able to do this with a minimal reduction in headcount – and that felt incredibly rewarding for me."

So we see that some Consultants really enjoy focusing on a diverse array of issues within a geographic region, while others prefer to focus on the industry first and dive deep into the issues seen at a single site.

One of the things I take away from these interviews is that **Consulting offers a wide range of options.** It's like a career buffet, where you can pick the items you find most appealing, and avoid the ones you find least interesting. Over time, as you find out which items in the buffet make you happiest, you can go back for seconds, thirds, etc. I like this idea of having a career that provides you the luxury of perusing all the options, as well as diving deeper once you get a sense of what you like.

So far, we have talked about what Consultants do, what their lives look like, and what their projects entail. From all of that, you may already have a sense about whether or not you would enjoy a career in Management Consulting. However, I also asked Veterans in Consulting their thoughts on other indications that you may love – or hate – about this career path. We'll look at their advice on this next.

Indications You May Love (or Hate) Consulting

When I was on Active Duty, I had little (if any) idea about what I wanted to do in my civilian career. As a result, I'm always eager to ask Veterans to point out signs that a Veteran may love his/her new career. It's also helpful to know the indications that they may hate that career as well. While nothing beats some hands-on experience, my intention in asking this is to help Veterans identify – or rule out – a potential career as quickly as possible.

Each of the Veterans I interviewed had something different to say on this, but here are some of the trends I saw. **The first aspect that may be appealing is a significant amount of variety in one's career.** Eric Hulbert told me:

> "Day-to-day life in consulting can vary a great deal. That's one of the things that people love about consulting – the variety. Your days are not necessarily alike, your cases are rarely all that similar, there's a ton of variety in what sorts of problems you're solving – what type of client you're doing with, what level of person you're dealing with, what level of interaction with the client."

For those who get bored easily, or are always wanting to learn something new, **Consulting can provide an endless stream of excitement, challenge, and growth. It can provide extravagant travel to every corner of the world, and the ability to spend an entire career never doing the same thing twice.** Trevor Miller put it this way:

> "A lot of the appeal of Consulting is that you get to work on very interesting problems. Especially for Veterans who may not know exactly what you want to go into, Management Consulting offers the opportunity to work on the cutting edge

of many different companies. That was a reason why I pursued it so much."

It's not just variety in the type of work you are doing, but **there is also an incredible diversity in the types of people with whom you will work.** As Tom Spahn shared:

"Less than half the people I work with have some sort of traditional business background. There are lawyers, tons of Veterans, teachers, a music PhD... pretty much every possible background you can imagine. And everyone brings something different to the team, and has a very different approach to looking at and solving a problem."

I asked Eric Hulbert what he thought might be an indication for someone on Active Duty that they might love Consulting, and he told me:

"If you're the type of person who is an over-achiever who constantly thinks that you're not doing enough, that's a personality trait you see a lot in consultants. Because you're having to produce a high impact in a very short amount of time, and so you need to be very conscientious that you are covering every possible detail – and there are many, many details."

For those on Active Duty interested in Consulting, Tom Spahn felt the best way to get a feel for if you would like Consulting is to start doing practice Case Problems online or in a book:

"If you start do these problems and you really like the exercise and the process, that is a clear sign that you would enjoy the type of thinking that is required as a Consultant."

I also learned about several indications that consulting might not be ideal for a Veteran. **One potential downside is that Consultants are most often in an advisory capacity, rather than an execution or implementation capacity.** The latter is most familiar to Veterans, who, on average, excel at both operations and implementing. Trevor Miller spoke to this when he shared:

> "What I would caution people to also think about is to make sure that these types of problems and structures appeal to you. For example, does being an Advisor rather than an Operator appeal to you? You could offer a solution to a client but they might ultimately not go that route and you have no say in that. Another difficult thing is when a client says that they are going to pursue it and then you leave but you never get to stay and see how it turns out. For me, I like that process. But if you're interested in learning about things in greater depth, it might not be the best fit for you."

In this respect, many Consulting projects end at the point where a typical Veteran may actually most enjoy the work. After having identified a solution to a complex problem, the work of rolling-up-ones-sleeves and getting to work is the responsibility of the client. This may prove frustrating to many Veterans who enjoy "making things happen."

One aspect that I've found consistent in my interviews with *Beyond the Uniform* is that **Veterans are often disappointed with the amount of time it takes for them to reach a senior level of leadership consistent with their military experience.** Many of the interviews I have conducted were with Veterans who entered into an industry or functional role that was not related or adjacent to their military experience. In this sense, a step back is almost always necessary.

With Consulting, this does not appear to be different (although this may vary if you enter into a consulting company known for military or government contract-related work). This was one of the first things that Kristen Sproat Colley pointed out to me:

> "I think one of the common misconceptions for Veterans coming into Consulting is that in the military they are used to leading people, doing problem solving, [and] running operations. But your first year in Consulting is not that.

You're getting an understanding of how the firm works. You're digging into data and refining presentations. Sometimes that adjustment is tough for Veterans. Plus, you don't have people working for you anymore. It takes a couple years to get back to a management level.

Veterans sometimes think that because they did all these great things in the military, they should automatically start at a higher level. But the truth is, we're really good at some stuff but we suck at other stuff. You have to start from the ground up and build your skillset within the industry."

It can be difficult to rule out career options while on Active Duty, but Eric Hulbert offered one way to use one's past experience to determine if Consulting might be a good fit:

"If you've never been excited by work, or if you've never enjoyed having an assignment in school that is ambiguous and difficult, then this is not for you."

Although the military offers a significant amount of uncertainty in terms of life-or-death situations, there is still a high degree of certainty in terms of job security, established career paths, and structured organizations. Tom Spahn spoke to this when he offered:

"If you don't like ambiguity, and not having control over the process, that can be very difficult. It is a client services industry where you own the deliverable the output, but 90% of your job is to convince people that you are suggesting the right things. That can be really rewarding, but it can also be really challenging at times when you absolutely know beyond the shadow of a doubt that you are suggesting something that will benefit the company, but for whatever reason the individual or the business unit you're dealing with has different priorities."

Every career has its pros and cons. **What's most important is that you identify your unique interests, likes and dislikes, and try to**

find a career that maximizes the positives for your personality and minimizes the downside.

At this point, you have a fair amount of information to evaluate whether Management Consulting would be compatible with your skills, desires, and ambitions. Next, let's look at the types of career paths that a career in Management Consulting can provide.

Common Career Paths

There are two common career paths for those in Management Consulting: you can remain in Consulting and work your way towards a Partner position, or you can transition to an industry – virtually any industry – when you are ready to move on. Let's start by looking at what it looks like if you remain in consulting for your entire career.

Blake Lindsey described the typical progression path like this:

> "Within Management Consulting we are a firm, so it is similar to what you might expect for a law firm. As a Consultant, your typical path is driving towards becoming a Partner. You are developing your skill set and moving along the ladder of developing clients, creating opportunities for others, [and] developing a core set of knowledge or skills that becomes marketable for our firm. And then the board would elect you to become a Partner. Start to finish, this will typically take about seven years."

Kristen went in-depth to highlight the differences in each career progression step:

> "For people who stay in Consulting, you start as the person that's putting together the slides and doing the analysis. Then you move into your first Management role where you have a few people under you. After that, you move into the sales side of things where you're working on bringing business to the firm. Finally, you become a Partner in the firm where you're managing the client relationships. The timeline to reach Partner is about ten years, but can be shorter or longer."

Trevor also detailed the standard times it takes to reach each promotion point. Consulting companies can be notorious for an "up or out" policy, where you either perform and are advanced, or are forced out of the company. However, provided that you are able to perform and grow in your role, the path to upward mobility is fairly straightforward and standardized. He explained:

> "Your first role is as an individual contributor responsible for one aspect of the client deliverable. You may be responsible for one or two Associates, but for the most part you are just an individual contributor. You'll be in this role for two to three years – two would be very fast, and three is more the norm. Then you become a Manager where you are running a team, and are responsible for the overall deliverable to the client. You'll work as a Manager for two to three years as well. From there, you become a Principal (also called an Associate Partner at some firms) where you are managing multiple teams and starting to be responsible for bringing in new business. This position is generally for two to three years as well. From there you would become a Partner, where you will manage multiple teams, bring in new business, but also start contributing to the firm's intellectual property based on the expertise you have accumulated in your career."

The second option is to pursue a career at a company after mastering a set of consulting skills. One of the advantages of a career in Consulting is that it can lead to virtually any follow-up career, often in a more senior position than could have been achieved if the Veteran went directly to this company. As Blake explains:

> "For the folks that take off-ramps, it's really great because Management Consulting is a highly-regarded career path. People that are leaving are coveted in *any* industry. I see people who go into just about anything: Private Equity, Entrepreneurship, Education, working to solve big problems in the public sector and with government, run big strategic groups at Amazon or Uber. It's very, very broad."

Tom Spahn spoke to the very high turnover rate associated with most top-tier consulting companies:

"The average tenure is about two years. It's not looked down upon to leave, and it's something we talk about very openly as we consider if we'd be happier continuing in Consulting or if it is time to move onto something else. But I think more than any other career path, Consulting offers the most variety in the options you can pursue after Consulting. You have so much exposure to so many different industries and so many different functional areas that it's easy to join another company, start a company, or do pretty much anything after you're ready to move on from Consulting."

Kristen echoed this sentiment:

"It's quite common that people leave Consulting after getting a few years of experience. I've seen a lot of people working in Operations roles. Some people move into Corporate Strategy roles. Many people also go into start-ups. These are the main exit points that I've seen for people leaving consulting."

One observation that I have made in the interviews I've conducted is that Veterans (and civilians too, for that matter) no longer have *Beyond the Uniform* direct and simple career paths. **Nearly every Veteran I've interviewed has worked in a variety of roles or industries prior to finding their ideal career path.** Viewed through this lens, I appreciate that the Consulting career path enables Veterans to gain a lot of experience as well as unlock a lot of doors to what may be their next ideal career.

Now that we've covered what Consultants do, what their life looks like, and what long-term career prospects are possible, let's next consider how to go about getting your foot in the door at a consulting company.

Applying

While each of the people I interviewed had advice to share with Veterans about how to apply for a job in Consulting, the first piece of advice was the most expedient: **plan in advance**. Trevor Miller advised:

> "First of all, on a logistical level, start early. I was blown away by how much effort was required to transition. Don't forget about how much time this will take to make these preparations. Many schools and jobs have timelines that are outside your control, and if you don't think about it early enough, you run the risk of missing a deadline."

Blake Lindsay said something very similar:

> "The process is long and drawn-out, so I encourage you to get involved early. Many Veterans have financial and family constraints, and don't give themselves the room necessary to go through a drawn-out interview process."

In addition to advising Veterans to start early, Kristen Sproat Colley also advises Veterans to **cast a wide net and use your connections to help you**. As she reflected on her own experience, she said:

> "When I started doing my research, I narrowed down my search to 5 firms I was interested in working for. I went to a Service Academy career fair and I was able to chat directly with 2 out of the 5 firms. I also identified people I knew working at those companies who were able to introduce me to others. I had one friend that I had deployed with that helped get me up to speed with the interview process."

Eric Hulbert, who transitioned to The Boston Consulting Group from his role at Bank of America, had some great advice about how to get your foot in the door – and echoes Kristen's networking advice:

"Management Consulting is unlike most other areas in that the recruiting process is highly defined. It's almost entirely based on recruiting from top-tier undergraduate, graduate, and PhD programs. So, breaking in from the outside requires a large amount of networking. The way that I did it was through friends. I started out by shooting for the stars, and saying I wanted to go to The Big Three. And I started looking on LinkedIn and saying, 'Who do I know at those firms?' and started reaching out to them. I did my research beforehand about what they did there, and showed them that I knew what was going on and was serious about a career in this industry. All I was looking for was advice on how to get my name in the pipeline."

This last piece of advice is consistent not just with the interviews I've conducted with Veterans in Consulting, but also in virtually every field. **One of the biggest assets you have in your career search is to reach out to fellow Veterans at the institution to which you are applying.** Not only can they provide you with extremely pertinent advice about how to explain your background and keys to success at each step of the process, but they may be able to help get your application in front of key decision-makers.

Another consistent piece of feedback the Veterans I interviewed shared about **common mistakes that military applicants make** is this: they do not adequately translate their military experience to a civilian hiring audience. Here's what Trevor had to say:

"For Veterans, the single biggest hurdle is translating your accomplishments from what you did in the military to what you want to do in the civilian sector. You take for granted that other people will understand what you have done. Being in the military for any amount of time, you assume that people will know, for example, what a deployment is like. But that's not normally general knowledge. So being able to take those experiences and translate that is key."

Kristen echoed this:

"A lot of people will say 'I did X, Y, and Z' instead of saying 'I am skilled at A, B, and C, because I did X, Y, and Z.' You need to translate what you did into what you can do and what you are now capable of. That's a huge step toward getting your foot in the door with a consulting firm, or any other company for that matter. I also prepared myself for the interview process, which is different than a standard job interview. I talked to Veterans that were already in my target firms and then went from there."

In my conversation with Trevor, he gave a fantastic example of what this might look like:

"My last job in the Marines – I was a Force Reconnaissance Platoon Commander. One of our obligations was to be the Crisis Response Force for the Marine Corps in the Western Hemisphere. I was very proud to serve in that role, but if I said that during an interview, it might not translate. So, what I did was drill that down into more specific pieces. For example, I met with senior executives and described our status and mission plans. At the same time, I prepared my Marines and explained the mission to them. When I focused in on my comfort with communicating with senior leaders or with my team, I think that resonated much more in an interview."

Another common mistake that military applicants make – in Consulting applications and beyond – is that **they don't adequately speak to their accomplishments in the military**. In the military community, the norm is to speak to your team's or unit's accomplishments, but never boast about your own achievements. While this works well within the Armed Forces, it will prove to be an enormous liability in your civilian career. You will be interviewing against civilians who have no problem (and significant experience) boasting about their accomplishments.

In order to remain competitive, you'll need to **find a way to speak to what you accomplished in the military, without taking it too far and becoming too boastful**. Here's what Trevor had to share:

"I would also advise you not to sell yourself short. When I was writing my resume and in my early networking stages, I had a tendency to downplay my accomplishments because in the military there is a culture that your accomplishments are because of your team. So, I didn't feel comfortable always saying that we were the best at something. But in the business world that's not perceived as humility, it's perceived as not being successful. So, I think it ends up hurting a lot of Veterans who are afraid to speak about their accomplishments."

One other piece of advice was to make sure that you **tailor your resume specifically to Consulting**. A resume that will work well for a role at Amazon will not be effective when applying to Consulting. As Trevor put it:

"Your resume has to be tailored to both the role and the company that you are going after. Not only are you describing things in a way that makes sense to them, but you're also highlighting things that are important to that company.

An example of this is being able to highlight your leadership impacts, especially as an Officer. At a very young age, you get the opportunity to lead large amounts of people. So, I would encourage people to focus on highlighting those types of things."

Once you are able to get an interview at a consulting company, the next step is to start preparing for the interview process. We'll look at this in the next chapter.

Interviewing

For such a highly demanding career option, you can imagine how difficult the interview process is. Not to worry – countless Veterans have gone before you and demonstrated that this can be done – it just takes a bit of preparation. Kristen Sproat Colley mentioned doing 30-40 different practice "Case Interviews" with friends and other Veterans in Consulting. Blake Lindsay spoke of going through 9 different interviews as part of his hiring process. Eric Hulbert talked about preparing for his interview for over four months to get his role at The Boston Consulting Group. Trevor put it succinctly:

> "As far as interviews, I would say that the biggest thing is repetitions. I read four different books including *Case in Point* and *Crack the Case*. I also ran 60 practice cases before I did my first interview. If I hadn't done that much preparation, I think I would have failed."

The good news is that Consulting interviews are highly standardized. Kristen gave a fantastic overview:

> "For the interview itself, there are two parts – the case interview and the fit interview. The fit interview is more similar to a traditional interview. The case interview is a bit different. The interviewer will give you a very generic question [or scenario]. For example, 'Our client is interested in sending people into space for a 15-minute tourist excursion.' And then you will need to discuss things like how this would be accomplished, how much the company should charge customers, etc. What this does is force you to break down a problem and ask the right questions to get to a solution. There were a couple books that I read to prepare as well as doing a whole bunch of practice cases." [NOTE: See the Resources section for a complete list of all book recommendations.]

One good thing about your preparation for the interview, as well as the interview itself, is that the Case Interview process is highly representative of what it is like to be a Consultant. So, if you enjoy this sort of exercise, it is actually a great indication that you may find a career in Consulting extremely fulfilling. Eric Hulbert explained this succinctly:

> "The Case Study is basically an entire Consulting project in 25 minutes or less. You walk through a hypothesis-driven approach to solving a problem in under a half-hour. It's more about solving a problem in a linear and logical manner and adequately communicating that you are doing that, so they understand what steps that you are taking."

Tom Spahn shared a similar experience:

> "The Case Study is very representative of the type of work you will do as a Consultant. For example, they may ask you, 'If you have a client whose company is suffering some sort of profitability drop... why is that?' And it's learning to take that question and ask the right follow-up questions and craft a solution. It's very much a co-creation with the interviewer where you problem solve with the interviewer as part of your team."

Here's how Kristen put it:

> "That process of figuring out what data you need, breaking down a problem, [and] finding possible solutions can also be a good indicator of whether or not you'll like that kind of analysis and problem-solving work. That process of problem solving that you need when doing the case interview is similar to what I now find myself using during different assignments."

If this whole process sounds intimidating, don't let that deter you! Trevor shared some words of encouragement:

> "If you're going down this road and preparing for a Consulting interview, don't be discouraged by feeling like you're not good at the case interview. I went through the

process myself and over the course of the past few months, I've helped others prepare as well. As far as I can tell, people aren't really natural at the process. For me, I had moments where I thought my preparation might be a waste of time because I wasn't smart enough to work in Consulting. But the more you prepare, the more comfortable you will become. It starts to be formulaic. All the case interview is doing is simulating solving a problem collaboratively. It was not until I reached a certain point that I really felt comfortable and understood the framework."

That's something any Veteran can do, right?
Right!

Over the last several chapters, we've taken a look at the ins-and-outs of what it's like to be a Consultant, as well as how to get and prepare for your interview. In the remaining chapters, we'll now shift gears and start to take a look at the quantitative side of Consulting and the Veterans who pursue a career in this industry.

The Top Ten

To better understand how and where military Veterans work within Management Consulting, I analyzed over 4300 LinkedIn profiles of Veterans who work in Management Consulting.

I started with Forbes's list of the *Ten Most Prestigious Management Consulting Companies*. Their ranking is based on a survey of 9000 Consultants at 65 North American firms, who were asked to rank their peers and competitors.

Whenever you consider a list of the "Top 10" variety, you should take it with a grain of salt – the exact ordering of these firms may vary (based on who is conducting the survey and when the survey takes place). It also overlooks smaller, boutique consulting firms (like Oliver Wyman) that have exceptional reputations but are designed to operate at a much smaller scale than consulting monoliths in the industry.

However, as a quantitative exercise in looking at where U.S. Military Veterans work within the field of Management Consulting, Forbes's list was a good starting point. It is also worth noting that the top three firms in their list – McKinsey & Company, the Boston Consulting Group, and Bain & Company – are commonly referred to as "The Big Three" (or "MBB"), as they are consistently the world's three largest consulting firms (as measured by revenue).

Here is Forbes's list:
1. McKinsey & Company
2. The Boston Consulting Group (BCG)
3. Bain & Company
4. Deloitte
5. Booz Allen
6. PricewaterhouseCoopers (PwC)
7. EY (formerly Ernst & Young)
8. Accenture
9. KPMG
10. IBM

At which companies do Veterans work?

Let's start with a look at where U.S. Military Veterans work within this grouping of ten Management Consulting companies. Based on the 4300 LinkedIn Profiles I studied, here's what I found:

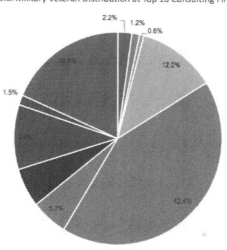

U.S. Military Veteran Distribution at Top 10 Consulting Firms

■ McKinsey ■ BCG ■ Bain ■ Deloitte ■ Booz Allen ■ PwC ■ EY ■ Accenture ■ KPMG ■ IBM

Figure 1 – The highest number of Veterans in consulting work at Booz Allen, followed by IBM, Deloitte, and Accenture.
(For a color version of this chart, please visit BeyondTheUniform.io/consulting-charts)

It is worth noting that many firms (including Booz Allen Hamilton, IBM and Deloitte) have many non-Consulting roles, which may be skewing these numbers.

Here are my main takeaways from this data:

- Less than 4% of all Veterans who go into Management Consulting end up at a Top 3 firm. If that is your aspiration, it would be worthwhile to study those who have gone before you and learn from how they got there. [NOTE: We will dive into that in the next chapter.]

- The largest Veteran populations are at Booz Allen Hamilton (42%), IBM (18%), Deloitte (12%), and Accenture (10%). These would be great firms for a military Veteran to consider, given the large pool of fellow Veterans from which to receive advice and assistance in applying, as well as a seemingly higher likelihood of being hired by one of these organizations.

Which branches of military service are represented at each company?

The next aspect I considered was how a Veteran's branch of military service impacts the Management Consulting firm at which he/she works.

Branch of Military Service for Veterans in Management Consulting

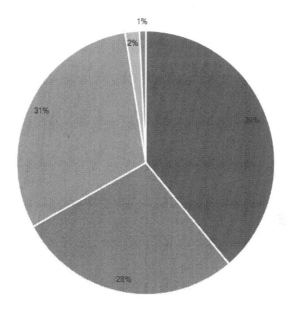

  US Army   US Navy   US Air Force   US Coast Guard   US Marine Corps

Figure 2 – The Army is most represented in Consulting, followed by the Air Force, Navy, Coast Guard, and then Marines.
(For a color version of this chart, please visit BeyondTheUniform.io/consulting-charts)

Here are my main takeaways:

- All branches of the U.S. military are well represented in the field of Management Consulting. If you are a member of the Armed Forces and you are interested in this industry, the branch of your service does not appear to play a significant factor in how each company will view your application.
- The Army dominates Management Consulting in terms of sheer numbers (39%). However, adjusted for population, a higher percentage of Navy and Air Force Veterans enter into Consulting than Army Veterans (0.7% for Navy & Air Force as compared to 0.5% for the Army).
- The Coast Guard and Marine Corps are smaller branches of service, so their smaller presence in Consulting was

expected. However, adjusted for population, their percentage was still smaller (0.3% for Coast Guard and 0.03% for Marine Corps Veterans).

- I found it interesting, amongst the branches, to see where each branch spiked in the population of a firm. For example, at McKinsey & Company, the Navy is actually the largest population – 44% vs. the Army's 40%. IBM has a fairly equal distribution of employees amongst the Army, Navy, and Air Force (33% / 32% / 33%). And Bain had an extreme number of Army Veterans, with 51% of their Veteran employees from the Army.

How will the length of military service affect a Consulting career?

I next looked at how the length of one's military service correlates to a career in Management Consulting.

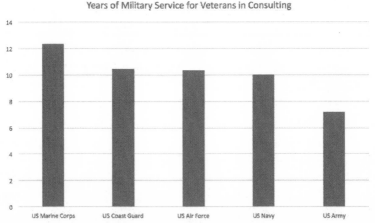

Figure 3 – Army Veterans in Consulting serve the shortest average amount of time in the military, while Marines serve the longest.

Across all branches of service, the average Veteran in Management Consulting serves in the military for **9.2** years. I found it more interesting, however, to look at how the length of military service varies by the consulting firm at which the Veteran works.

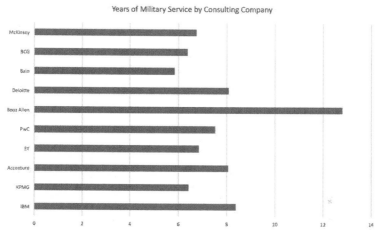

Figure 4 – The average length of a Veteran's military service based on the consulting company at which he/she works.

My main takeaways from this are:

- Military Veterans who work at a Top 3 Management Consulting company serve in the military for 24% less time than those at other consulting companies. In the next chapter, we will look at how an MBA is the most common route to one of The Big Three. One potential explanation, then, for the shorter length of service for those Veterans at The Big Three is that it is easier for a Veteran to pursue an MBA earlier in his/her career, when the opportunity, cost, and life obligations are likely to be lower.
- The top three highest employers of Veterans – Booz Allen Hamilton, IBM, and Deloitte – also had the highest lengths of service (12.8, 8.4, and 8.1 years of military service, respectively).

How will the length of civilian work experience affect a Consulting career?

While the length of one's military service is a factor to consider, the other aspect I looked at was how much civilian work experience a Veteran had prior to joining a Management Consulting company. For this, I measured the length of time between the end of one's military service and the start of his/her Consulting career. The duration of this time might entail time spent unemployed, time spent employed at another company, and/or time spent at college or graduate school.

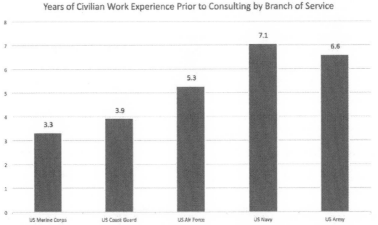

Years of Civilian Work Experience Prior to Consulting by Branch of Service

Figure 5 – Navy Veterans have the longest average length of civilian work experience prior to consulting, while Marines have the shortest.

There seems to be a relationship between length of military service and length of civilian experience. While U.S. Marines had the longest length of military service prior to entering into Consulting, they had the shortest length of civilian work experience prior to going into Management Consulting. Similarly, the Army had the shortest duration of military service, and were amongst the longest length of civilian work experience.

I then looked at how this varied by individual consulting company.

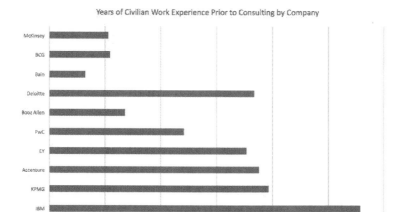

Figure 6 – The average length of a Veteran's civilian work experience prior to working in Consulting.

Here is what stood out to me:

- The Big Three – McKinsey, BCG, and Bain – had civilian work experience trends highly correlated to the average length of time to pursue an MBA (2.1, 2.2 and 1.3 years of experience respectively).
- Booz Allen Hamilton averaged just 2.7 years of work experience. You'll recall that Booz Allen had the longest length of military service, at 12.7 years. So I would guess that people spend more time on Active Duty prior to working at Booz Allen, but more often go directly from the military to work there.

This also made me curious to look at the total amount of experience – both military and civilian – that a Veteran has before entering into Management Consulting. Here's what I found:

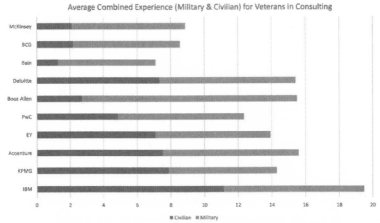

Figure 7 – The total average length of both civilian and military experience for Veterans based on the consulting company at which they work.
(For a color version of this chart, please visit BeyondTheUniform.io/consulting-charts)

What are the common job titles and salaries?

The last two factors I considered were the most common job titles and their corresponding salaries, according to Glassdoor.com. I looked at total compensation (base salary and all bonuses), and used Glassdoor salary information using San Francisco as the location for salary comparison.

One quick disclaimer: there are so many factors to consider when selecting a job – location, responsibilities, cultural fit, opportunity for advancement, etc. Salary is one of the easiest to quantify, but is not the most important factor to consider. My intention in delving into this data was merely to provide Veterans with more information so that they can make a decision that is right for them.

Here are the top 10 things I found when it came to salary:

1. The highest salary went to Accenture, where the most common title for military Veterans is Senior Manager, which has a total annual salary of $207K.

2. McKinsey, the Boston Consulting Group, and Bain all had comparable titles (Associate for McKinsey, and Consultant for BCG & Bain), with corresponding annual salaries of $180K.
3. IBM's most common job title was Managing Consultant, which has an average annual salary of $144K.
4. Booz Allen Hamilton has the most common title of Associate, with a corresponding annual salary of $132K.
5. Deloitte's most common title was Senior Consultant, with a corresponding salary of $127K.
6. PWC's most common title is Senior Associate, which has a salary of $104K.
7. EY's most common title for Veterans is Senior Consultant, with an average annual salary of $102K.
8. KPMG's most common title is Senior Associate and a salary of $91K.

The final way I wanted to look at this data was by looking at the combined years of experience – both military and civilian – and seeing how much salary you get per year of experience. Seen in this light, the best deal is with Bain & Company, which is the highest at $24K per year of experience. BCG and McKinsey were a close second, both providing $20.5K per year of experience. And Accenture came in at #4 with $13K per year of experience.

Now that we've looked at the career landscape from the perspective of a "Top Ten" approach, let's zoom in and take a look at what we can learn from Veterans who work at one of The Big Three (also called "MBB").

The Big Three

In the previous chapter, we looked at over 4300 LinkedIn profiles to learn of the trends amongst military Veterans who work as Management Consultants. In this research, we saw that less than 4% of all military Veterans within the field of Management Consulting work at "The Big Three" – McKinsey & Company, The Boston Consulting Group, and Bain & Company. That made me curious to learn **what set this batch apart**, and what someone might consider if he/she is a military Veteran desiring to work at The Big Three.

Branches of Military Service Represented at The Big Three

The first thing I looked into was how a military Veteran's branch of service correlates to his/her working at The Big Three. I also wanted to delve into the length of one's military service prior to entering into Management Consulting.

Here's what I found:

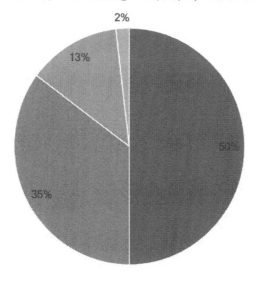

Veterans at a Top 3 Consulting Company by Branch of Service

2%
13%
50%
35%

■ Army ■ Navy ■ Air Force ■ Marine Corps ■ Coast Guard

Figure 8 – Army Veterans make the biggest cohort at The Big Three, followed by the Navy, and then distantly the Air Force and Marine Corps.
(For a color version of this chart, please visit BeyondTheUniform.io/consulting-charts)

Every branch of the Armed Services is currently represented at The Big Three, with the exception of the U.S. Coast Guard. If you're in the Coast Guard, don't let that deter you – this has not historically been the case, but was so at the time that I analyzed this data.

The Army dominates The Big Three, making up half of the Veteran population there, followed closely by the Navy and distantly by the Air Force and Marine Corps. This is true even when you adjust for the relative populations amongst the branches.

Average Length of Military Service for Veterans at The Big Three

Next, I wanted to see how long Veterans served in the military prior to joining The Big Three.

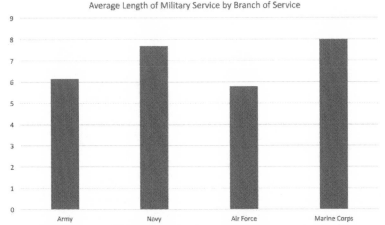

Average Length of Military Service by Branch of Service

Figure 9 – Marines at The Big Three have the longest average length of military service, while the Air Force has the shortest.

Across all branches, the average Veteran served in the military for **6.7** years prior to joining The Big Three. This seemed to indicate that most Veterans served for their initial 4-5 year commitment as well as a follow-up "shore tour." It is also clear that most Veterans at The Big Three exited the military early in their career.

Common Routes from Active Duty to The Big Three

Next, I was curious about the way in which Veterans made their way to The Big Three. To look at this, I categorized the route taken into one of three paths:

1. **School** – the Veteran attended an undergraduate or graduate school program immediately preceding their joining one of The Big Three.
2. **Direct** – the Veteran went directly from military service into one of The Big Three.
3. **Industry** – the Veteran worked at another civilian company prior to joining one of The Big Three. This could be at another Management Consulting firm, or a company in an entirely different industry.

Please note that I only considered what the Veteran was doing **immediately** prior to starting at one of The Big Three. For example, if a Veteran went from Active Duty into an industry, then went to a school, and then to one of The Big Three, I still classified their route as "School." Similarly, if a Veteran went to school, then to a job, and then to Consulting, their route would be classified as "Industry."

Here is what I found:

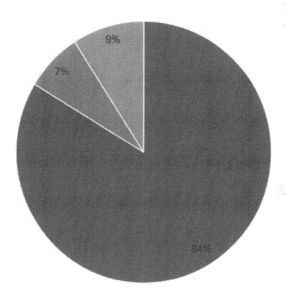

The Route Military Veterans Take to a Top 3 Consulting Company

■ School   ■ Direct   ■ Industry

Figure 10 – The overwhelming majority of Veterans at The Big Three go there directly from school.
(For a color version of this chart, please visit BeyondTheUniform.io/consulting-charts)

The overwhelming majority of Veterans at The Big Three went to school prior to joining the consulting company. Only 7% of Veterans were able to make a direct transition from Active Duty to an MBB, which speaks to how difficult that route is.

When we look at the average length of military service for these Veterans, as classified by the route they took to an MBB, it becomes more interesting:

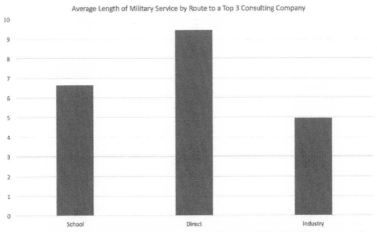

Average Length of Military Service by Route to a Top 3 Consulting Company

Figure 11 – Veterans who go directly from the military to The Big Three serve for the longest average amount of time in the military, while those who go to Consulting from an industry serve the shortest amount of time.

The rare few who are able to transition directly to an MBB served on Active Duty for 42% longer than those who went to school and 91% longer than those who went to work in industry. Those Veterans who worked at another civilian company prior to joining an MBB served the shortest amount of time, at an average of 5 years of service. I interpreted this to mean that they served the minimum length of service (the vast majority of profiles viewed were Officers) prior to starting their civilian career.

Highest Level of Education for Veterans at The Big Three

Given how many Veterans pursued schooling prior to entering into an MBB, I then considered the highest level of education achieved for those working at The Big Three. Please note that some Veterans hold multiple advanced degrees. Also, some Veterans may have achieved their highest level of education while at the consulting company. However, given (1) that a Master's degree or higher is a stated requirement for each of these firms, and (2) the demanding schedule associated with Consulting, I don't believe it is likely that the Veteran advanced his/her education while working at an MBB.

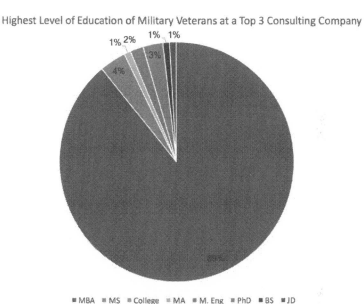

Figure 12 – The overwhelming majority of Veterans at The Big Three have an MBA. (For a color version of this chart, please visit BeyondTheUniform.io/consulting-charts)

Amongst all Veterans working at The Big Three, the overwhelming majority (89%) have an MBA. It is also worth noting that, although an advanced degree is stated as a job requirement, 1% of Veterans hold a BSc with no indication of an advanced degree on their LinkedIn profiles.

To add more color to this information, I wanted to see how this varied based on the route the Veteran took to get to The Big Three.

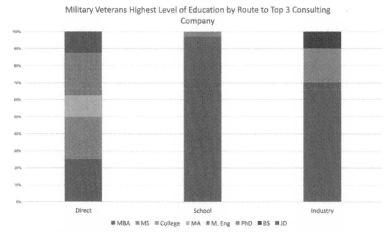

Military Veterans Highest Level of Education by Route to Top 3 Consulting Company

■ MBA ■ MS ■ College ■ MA ■ M. Eng ■ PhD ■ BS ■ JD

Figure 13 – The breakdown of highest level of education for Veterans at The Big Three based on the route they took to get there.
(For a color version of this chart, please visit BeyondTheUniform.io/consulting-charts)

While most Veterans at The Top Three have an MBA, it is **most true** for those Veterans who proceeded to The Big Three directly from school (where 97% of all Veterans earned an MBA) and **least true** of Veterans who went directly from the military to The Big Three (where only 25% hold an MBA).

It is also worth noting that there was the most diversity of education in those Veterans who went to The Big Three directly from the military. While this comprises only 7% of profiles analyzed, I did not see the lopsidedness towards an MBA that I did amongst the "school" (97% MBA) or "industry" (70% MBA) routes.

Most Common MBA Programs for Veterans at The Big Three

Given the high number of Veterans with MBA degrees at The Big Three, the last aspect I researched was the schools the Veterans chose to pursue their MBAs at, prior to working at The Big Three.

Here are the top MBA programs I found:

1. Harvard Business School (20%)
2. The Wharton School of the University of Pennsylvania (15%)
3. MIT Sloan School of Management (7%)
4. University of Virginia Darden School of Business (7%)
5. The University of Chicago Booth School of Business (6%)
6. The Stanford Graduate School of Business (5%)
7. Northwestern's Kellogg School of Management (5%)
8. Duke's Fuqua School of Business (4%)
9. Dartmouth College's Tuck School of Business (3%)
10. Yale School of Management (3%)

It is worth noting that these numbers are not adjusted for class size, and that the Stanford Graduate School of Business (the graduate school I attended), Northwestern's Kellogg School of Management, and Dartmouth College's Tuck School of Business all have class sizes approximately one-third of the others on this list.

Experiences of Veterans who Transitioned Directly from Active Duty to The Big Three

Given the apparent difficulty to go directly from Active Duty to a consulting role at an MBB, I wanted conclude with the experiences of two Veterans who managed to do this.

Kristen Sproat Colley said:

> "I got my Master's degree immediately after college, in Forced Migration Refugee Studies. The specific content of this degree doesn't really translate to my work at BCG, but the critical thinking skills definitely do. My last job in the Marine Corps was as an Information Operations Planner. So I was flying into different places and augmenting the staff on the ground to re-frame issues they were facing and coming up with solutions. I knew I really liked that kind of problem-solving.

When I was getting out of the military, I was considering going back to school. I learned about Consulting, and realized that it was a similar process to the thought process I used in the military. I think that experience was also ultimately critical to me being able to get the job. I was able to say 'I know how to look at a problem and break it down.' Also being able to translate my experience in the military to civilian terms and make it meaningful to a civilian organization [helped]. That's a huge step toward getting your foot in the door with a consulting firm, or any other company, for that matter. I also prepared myself for the interview process, which is different than a standard job interview. I talked to Veterans that were already in my target firms and then went from there.

Trevor Miller said:

"Nothing was done deliberately to make my transition directly to Bain & Company possible. The most immediate thing that helped was that I went to graduate school immediately after the Naval Academy. For those looking into Consulting, a graduate degree can be almost mandatory. I think this is a reason a lot of Veterans go to business school if they are interested in pursuing Consulting.

While my graduate degree was important, the things that I happened to do as an Infantry Officer and as a Force Reconnaissance Officer helped build skills that parallel what I now do as a Consultant. Particularly during my time as a Force Reconnaissance Officer, we weren't doing those deployments to Afghanistan and Iraq anymore. We were doing a lot of going to other countries and training with their Special Operations units. We would exchange techniques and also improve their processes and make them more effective allies of the United States. It was a pretty similar process to Management Consulting. It's going in, listening to what the problem or issue is, helping people think through them, and communicate a solution.

I actually thought about going to business school. It seemed like a path a lot of people took after the military. In particular, I was interested in Stanford's Graduate School of Business. I thought, 'This is the place for me.' I was interested in entrepreneurship and starting my own business. I called up a friend of mine who went to the Kennedy School with me. He later went on to Stanford GSB. He said to me, 'Well, what do you want to do after business school?' My first thought was Management Consulting, because I would have the opportunity to learn firsthand everything I had learned in business school. My friend told me that I could make the jump right away. I just found myself remembering the difference in my personal development from my time in graduate school compared with my time in the Marine Corps. So I came to the conclusion that if I could make the jump, I wanted to do that."

The Big Three are notoriously difficult places to be accepted and going directly from Active Duty to them is even more difficult still. However, I am an adamant believer that "success leaves clues." By studying the examples of Veterans at the exclusive Big Three, you can learn tactics that will help you in your pursuit of any consulting company. It bears repeating that one of the most effective tactics mentioned in my interviews was reaching out to and receiving advice from Veterans at the firm to which you are applying. I hope that the information above helps you prepare for those conversations, but does not relieve you of the need to have them.

We have now covered everything I have learned from my research, personal experience, and Veteran interviews. Let's wrap this all up in some final thoughts.

Conclusion

It can be extremely intimidating to select your first civilian career after serving in the military on Active Duty. I know that I was daunted by this transition, and I know that every single one of the 150+ Veterans I interviewed for *Beyond the Uniform* were intimidated by this as well.

I hope that this book has helped you better understand what a career in Management Consulting looks like, and has given you some initial indications of whether or not this would be a good career option for you. If it is, I hope it has given you the confidence to know that – should you set your sites on Consulting – **there is a clear path to get there and many Veterans are willing to help you along the way.**

One final story that I'll share is a lesson I learned five years after graduating from the Stanford Graduate School of Business. I – and each of my classmates at Stanford – spent hundreds of hours preparing our business school applications. We researched the career we wanted to pursue after business school, and wrote convincing essays speaking to our conviction about that career path. Then, once we got to business school, we changed our minds about our desired career, threw it out the window, and started researching a new career option! We furiously prepared for our summer internship interviews, once again convinced that we had figured out what we wanted to do.

Then, we went off to our summer internships, and over the course of ten-weeks, I – and, again, the overwhelming majority of my classmates – realized that we had gotten our ideal career wrong. So, we spent the majority of our second year at business school researching, identifying, and preparing for our first job out of business school. One year out of business school, the majority of my classmates had started a second job. Two years, the majority of my classmates were heading in another direction as well. At this point, nine years out from business school, a month doesn't go by where I talk with a classmate who is considering shifting their career!

I'm not sharing this story to intimidate you, but rather the opposite – to let you know that this is part of the process. If you start your civilian career and believe it is the end-all-be-all, it's highly likely that you're going to be disappointed when, at some point, you shift to a different career. **However, if you approach looking at a career in Consulting (or even if you approach starting your career in Consulting) as merely the first of many "lily pads" on your way to your ideal career path, I believe you'll be more realistic in your approach and more fulfilled in your results.**

From the 150+ interviews I've done with military Veterans I have seen, time and time again, that Veterans can do whatever it is they would like to do in their civilian careers. While I do believe that Management Consulting is an ideal career path for many Veterans, I also know that each of us is different in our abilities, desires, and ambitions. I hope this book has served as a resource towards your finding your ideal career.

There is no one who deserves that more than those who have served our country so selflessly.

Recommended Resources

The following is a list of resources if you would like to learn more about or start to prepare for a career in Management Consulting. This list is based on resources that have been recommended during my interviews.

- Service Academy Career Conference (SACC)
- Websites
  - Case Interview Secrets *(From a Former McKinsey Case Interviewer)* – *http://www.caseinterview.com/*
  - Understanding compensation
    - Charles Aris Strategy Consulting Compensation Study 2017: https://www.slideshare.net/AshleeWagner1/charles-aris-strategy-consulting-compensation-study-2017
    - GlassDoor – http://www.glassdoor.com
  - Management Consulted – https://managementconsulted.com/
  - MilitaryToBusiness – Admissions Consulting for Top Military Performers – offers business school consulting advice on how to shape your resume. They also have a blog with posts about when to make transition to business school and other similar topics. Even if you're not thinking of business school, they have high-quality, free content.
  - Personal Experience Interview
  - McKinsey Operations Practice
- Books
  - Case Interview Secrets: A Former McKinsey Interviewer Reveals How to Get Multiple Job Offers in Consulting
  - Case In Point: Complete Case Interview Preparation
  - Crack the Case System: How to Conquer Your Case Interviews
- Relevant Podcast Interviews

- BTU #1 – Blake Lindsay: Active Duty to Consulting @ McKinsey & Company
- BTU #15 – Tom Spahn: Law School, Corporate Law, and Management Consulting
- BTU #29 – Eric Hulbert: Navy Aviation to BofA to the Boston Consulting Group
- BTU 143: Active Duty to Consultant at Bain & Company (Trevor Miller)
- BTU #144 – Active Duty to the Boston Consulting Group (Kristen Sproat Colley)
- BTU #12 – Tim Avery: Consulting, the PhD Process, and Self-Knowledge
- Videos
  - Veterans in Consulting Panel – a conversation with three Veterans who went directly from Active Duty to an MBB – http://beyondtheuniform.io/publications/Veterans-consulting-seminar/

About the Author

Justin M. Nassiri is the Founder & CEO of StoryBox, and started *Beyond the Uniform* as a side project to help active duty military personnel. With *Beyond the Uniform*, he has conducted over 150 interviews with military Veterans about their civilian careers: what they do, how they got there, and their advice to other Veterans. He has had the privilege of interviewing the CEO of Pepsi, NFL players, Academy Award nominees, and more.

He started out United States Naval Academy, where he studied Electrical Engineering. He also received the world's finest education in leadership, serving as the Brigade Performance and Conduct Officer and the President of the Men's Glee Club. (As a result, his wife Rebecca refers to herself as the First Lady.)

After the Naval Academy, Justin served as an Officer with the incredible crew of the USS Alaska (SSBN 732) and for a far-too-brief time with the USS Chicago. This training was the single biggest asset to his experience as an entrepreneur, helping him break through walls, push himself beyond his limits, and occasionally fight giant squid as well as flirt with mermaids.

His life was forever changed when he attended the Stanford Graduate School of Business. There, he learned that investment bankers weren't tellers at a bank (true story), that ordinary people can start baby companies called startups, and that if you're dressed in 70s attire on a flight to Vegas, you can get away with giving the safety announcement.

He has worked as a Consultant with McKinsey & Company at their New York Office. He also founded StoryBox, a marketing technology company that has raised over $3M in venture capital, and worked with over 35 Fortune 500 companies including Disney, Budweiser, and Microsoft.

58229063R00043

Made in the USA
Middletown, DE
05 August 2019